Translated by Rebecca Neal

Pantagruel
BY FRANÇOIS RABELAIS

Bright
≡Summaries.com

FRANÇOIS RABELAIS

FRENCH HUMANIST WRITER

- **Born in Chinon (France) in around 1494.**
- **Died in Paris in 1553.**
- **Notable works:**
  - *Pantagruel* (1532), novel
  - *Gargantua* (1534), novel
  - *The Third Book* (1546), novel

François Rabelais was born in around 1494. He was the son of a lawyer, but decided to take holy orders in around 1510. Men of letters, both monks and laymen, shared their passion for Antiquity and humanism with him.

Rabelais left the clergy in 1527 for unknown reasons and went to study medicine at the University of Montpellier. He then moved to Lyon, where he wrote humorous pamphlets and began to correspond with Erasmus (Dutch humanist, 1469-1536). He also published his first two books (*Pantagruel* and *Gargantua*), which were censored by the College of Sorbonne. Rabelais then became the secretary of Jean du Bellay (French bishop and diplomat, 1492/98-1560), who he accompanied to Rome. From 1546, he began to publish sequels to his books, a decision which caused him a lot of trouble with the Sorbonne. Some time later, the cardinal managed to get him the position of curate of Meudon, which he resigned from in 1553.

Rabelais was an original, cultivated and jovial man. He died in 1553 in Paris.

PANTAGRUEL

A HIGHLY COLOURFUL BOOK

- **Genre:** novel
- **Reference edition:** Rabelais, F. (2006) *Gargantua and Pantagruel*. Trans. Screech, M.A. London: Penguin.
- **1st edition:** 1532
- **Themes:** education, parody, Christianity, language, gigantism

Pantagruel is the first book in a series of five, alongside *Gargantua*, *The Third Book*, *The Fourth Book* and *The Fifth Book*. It recounts the adventures of a giant with an insatiable appetite (giving rise to the adjective Pantagruelian) who leaves his kingdom, Utopia, to study at various universities across France.

The book, which was written under the pseudonym Alcofribas Nasier (an anagram of François Rabelais) to avoid censorship, was a resounding success when it was first published in 1532, but was soon condemned by the Sorbonne (1534). Indeed, in this book, which is written using crude and direct language, Rabelais offers a meandering description of the society of his time and makes fun of his contemporaries and their knowledge.

SUMMARY

PROLOGUE

Rabelais addresses his readers and presents *Pantagruel* as a miracle cure for all illnesses.

CHAPTERS 1-22

The author sets out Pantagruel's origins by describing his entire family tree: he gives us a mixture of names from the Bible, classical mythology, and chivalric romances.

Badebec gives birth to Pantagruel (whose name means "all thirst", p. 24), as well as men, books and drinks, which is useful as they are in the middle of a drought. She dies in childbirth, leaving Pantagruel's father Gargantua perplexed: should he cry because his wife has died, or laugh because his son has been born? He chooses to make the most of his happiness, because crying will not bring his wife back.

Even though Pantagruel is still a child, he commits "the most terrible deeds" (p. 27): he escapes from his cradle even though he is chained to it and devours everything in his path, including the milk of hundreds of cows and the contents of an enormous trough. His education begins in Poitiers, and then he visits the universities of Bordeaux and Toulouse, where he learns dancing and sword fighting. Next, he goes to Montpellier to study medicine, but gives it up. On his way, he builds the Pont du Gard. His teacher Epistemon then takes him to Valence, Angers and Bourges, where he studies law. Finally, they go to Orleans.

On the way to Paris, Pantagruel meets a student who is showing off by speaking an incomprehensible jargon that is a mixture of Latin and French. He is quick to put the boy in his place. Before he reaches Paris, he also pulls off the feat of lifting a very heavy bell that has sunk into the ground. Once the Parisians find out about this, they all rush to see him. He visits the Library of Saint Victor, where he finds an impressive collection of books on a range of subjects, including law, theology and natural sciences.

Pantagruel receives a letter from his father explaining the importance of education, and in particular of language learning. Unlike Gargantua, Pantagruel is living in a new era with inventions that seem to come from "divine inspiration" (p. 47), such as printing.

Pantagruel sees an injured man and goes to talk to him. However, the man answers him in German. When the giant fails to understand him, the stranger tries a series of languages, including Spanish, Indian, Italian, Danish and Dutch. Eventually they understand one another in French. The stranger is called Panurge, and Pantagruel becomes friends with him.

Pantagruel organises public debates on the most obscure scientific subjects in order to test his knowledge. He shines as he takes on professors, students and theologians. Some university professors ask Pantagruel for his help in resolving a very complicated legal problem. The giant has to serve as the judge in a trial between two lords, le Sieur de Bumkis and le Sieur de Slurp-ffart. When Bumkis begins to talk, his speech is obscure and full of technical terms and wordplay. Slurp-ffart's language is just as impossible to understand. Pantagruel questions the scholars who are there, but none of them want to make a decision. They therefore leave the sentence up to the giant, who delivers his judgement in language that is just as outlandish as that of the two lords.

His judgement earns Pantagruel great renown. Meanwhile, Panurge recounts his misfortunes: he was taken prisoner by the Turks, who wanted to cook him, but he managed to escape by setting the town on fire. He criticises the walls of Paris, "since with a single fart a cow could blow down more than six arm-spans of them" (p. 81). He proposes building a new wall using "the thingummybobs of women" (ibid.).

Panurge always carries small purses filled with ingredients that he uses for his practical jokes, such as itching powder and things to stain clothes with. He is constantly short of money, and has no qualms about tricking or stealing from people. In addition, he has found a way of making money by stealing silver from relics. He also tells Pantagruel about his trials: in particular, he summoned women to court for wearing high-cut collars to stop men from touching them.

The English scholar Thaumaste has heard about Pantagruel's wisdom and wants to publicly debate with him, but only through signs. Panurge suggests standing in for his friend, convinced that "before all the world, I shall make him shit vinegar" (p. 101). The Englishman then begins miming and Panurge responds. The experts all interpret the "discussion" differently. Thaumaste then thanks Panurge and Pantagruel, and recognises their superior knowledge. As a result, Panurge also becomes famous in Paris. He approaches a high-ranking woman, but she rejects him and tells him to stop bothering her. Panurge tries in vain to seduce her with lavish gifts. He then gets back at her by sprinkling some powder on her dress; this immediately attracts dogs, which urinate on her.

CHAPTERS 22-34

Pantagruel returns to Utopia after the Dipsodes invade and drive Gargantua out. Before he sets off, Pantagruel receives a letter from a lover. Confused by the blank letter containing a gold ring, Pantagruel asks Panurge for help. They turn to books to find out why the ink has turned invisible, before finally realising that the text is engraved on the ring.

As soon as they arrive in Utopia, Pantagruel and Panurge are attacked by 600 horsemen. Panurge and his other companions burn them and take one prisoner. They then organise a feast, and Pantagruel interrogates the prisoner. He finds out that their enemy, King Anarch, has a vast army made up of giants led by Loup Garou, foot soldiers, pioneers, goblins, cannons and prostitutes.

Pantagruel puts up a monument to commemorate his companions' victory. He creates men and women by farting; he calls them pygmies and sends them to a nearby island.

Pantagruel releases the prisoner so that he can tell his people about his exploits, and gives him a drink to deliver to his king. When the king and his generals drink the liquid, they begin to suffer from an unquenchable thirst. Pantagruel then sends his companions to set fire to the enemy camp, before sprinkling it with salt and flooding it with his urine. The giants narrowly manage to save the king from drowning. Praying that God will protect him, Pantagruel then fights the giant Loup Garou, who invokes Muhammed.

Although he has won the battle, Pantagruel mourns his teacher Epistemon, whose head has been cut off. Nonetheless, Panurge manages to heal him. Now that he has come back to life, Epistemon recounts his journey to hell, where he met a range a range of real and fictional famous figures from Antiquity and the Middle Ages, as well as popes.

Pantagruel receives a hero's welcome in his homeland and sets out with some warriors to the land of the Dipsodes in order to start a colony. He punishes the King of the Dipsodes by turning him into a crier of green sauce and marrying him to an old woman.

The narrator, Alcofrybas Nasier, visits the inside of the giant, where there is a whole world with many towns and inhabitants.

Pantagruel falls ill: he is purged and people are sent to unblock his stomach.

The narrator promises that the next part of the story will be told at a coming fair and heralds the adventures to come. He finishes by criticising the people who read the book just so they can attack it.

CHARACTER STUDY

PANTAGRUEL

He is the giant son of Gargantua and Badebec. When he was born, he was already large, handsome and hairy. With his respect for familial duties and sense of honour, Pantagruel is always ready to help: for example, he builds a bridge, chases away brigands, puts a pedant in his place and pulls a bell out of the ground. To avoid disappointing his father, he studies diligently and tests his knowledge in public debates. His judgement is full of good sense and he displays "super-human wisdom" (p. 73). Even so, he is modest and does not think that he is perfect. He is very devout and illustrates Rabelais' ideas about religion.

GARGANTUA

Gargantua is Pantagruel's father and Badebec's husband. He attaches a great deal of importance to marriage and the continuation of the line. He represents traditional knowledge, which he criticises: he does not want his son to follow the same path. The letter he sends to Pantagruel can be seen as a sort of spiritual testament in which he explains the importance not only of universal knowledge, but also of the values and virtues to acquire (Chapter 8).

PANURGE

Panurge is originally from France, but was taken prisoner by the Turks and speaks many languages. He is friends with

Pantagruel, and is a bon vivant who appreciates all the pleasures in life: food, drink and sex. He is very interested in women, and has a long list of conquests. He is the character who is best described from a physical and psychological point of view: he is a thin, amiable, 35-year-old man of medium height with an aquiline nose. He is also a wanderer, a spendthrift and something of a thief. He is a mischievous character, and always carries little purses filled with ingredients that he uses for his practical jokes: he uses itching powder, stains fine clothes, farts and steals silverware (Chapter 16). He is ingenious and cunning, and comes to the aid of Pantagruel and his companions on several occasions: during the dispute against Thaumaste (Chapters 18-20), to solve the mystery of the invisible ink (Chapter 24), and during the battle against the Dipsodes, where he demonstrates his skills as a doctor.

ANALYSIS

EDUCATION

What makes a good education?

As a humanist, Rabelais attaches a great deal of importance to education and teaching, particularly of languages. The letter that Gargantua writes to his son to encourage him in his learning all over France (this is how people carried out their studies in the 16th century) is a good illustration of this: it serves as an argument in favour of a humanist education.

After criticising the teaching of the Middle Ages, Gargantua explains the importance of study to Pantagruel (and the reader). This will allow him to attain the Renaissance ideals of knowledge and virtue. His father encourages him to become "an abyss of erudition" (p. 49), meaning that he should acquire all the knowledge of the time. This includes ancient languages (Latin, Greek, Hebrew, Chaldean and Arabic), the seven liberal arts (fundamental knowledge in the Middle Ages comprising grammar, rhetoric, dialectics, arithmetic, music, geometry and astronomy), civil law, natural history, medicine, the art of war, biblical texts and ancient texts, in particular those of moralists like Plutarch. In this way, Rabelais conveys his message that a good education permits the acquisition of universal knowledge.

GOOD TO KNOW: HUMANISM

Humanism, which originated in Italy in the 13th century

before spreading across all of Europe until the 16th century, refers to a movement of total renewal in the arts and thought. Scholars left behind the legacy of the Middle Ages, which were seen as a "dark" period (p. 47), to bring back the knowledge of Antiquity (seen as a glorious past), put greater emphasis on man, who must be educated, and reconcile these two ideas with Christianity. It is worth noting that, in the case of Rabelais, specialists talk of Christian humanism: like other authors, he was very interested in religious questions, in particular the circulation of a translation of the Bible which remained faithful to the original text.

Educating the reader

Throughout the text, Rabelais tries to educate his reader. First of all, he incorporates elements from all of human knowledge in the 16th century into his novel:

- he makes many allusions to biblical characters (Noah, p. 15), men and heroes from Greek, Roman and Eastern Antiquity (Archimedes, p. 38; Ovid, p. 18; Aeneas and Dido, p. 122; Sennacherib, p. 140), authors and knights from the Middle Ages (François Villon, p. 152; King Arthur, p. 149) and humanists (Pico della Mirandola, p. 58);
- he puts forward a list of books that are classics in their domain (every time he is faced with a problem, Pantagruel turns to books, such as treatises on architecture and works on signs);
- he uses precise and specialised vocabulary, notably in the legal domain, and even explains some situations

linked to the law (in particular, he mocks legal jargon in Chapters 11-13) and medicine;

- he also deals with cultural elements that are directly inspired by everyday life: national prejudices (the inhabitants of Bourbon have big ears), the trades and their reputations (the pot-makers of Villedieu in Normandy) and popular common sense ("Did you understand all that? Then down a good swig without water! For if you believe it not, 'Neither do I,' said she", p. 21).

He also provides his contemporaries with *exempla*. These are real or fictional anecdotes about men or animals with a positive or negative moral, which Renaissance authors used to illustrate their ideas. They aim to teach by making the reader understand a concept and helping them to remember it. For example, Agesilaus serves as a reminder of the virtue of the Spartans (p. 80), and the story of the lion and the fox teaches the reader about the hygiene of wounds.

Finally, Rabelais also uses laughter to educate his readers. In doing so, he follows the Latin adage on comedy: *castigat mores ridendo* ("laughing corrects morals"). Laughter is therefore an educational tool which allows the author to gently denounce the failings of his contemporaries so that they can change their ways. Rabelais mainly uses:

- parody: his novel parodies chivalric romances (in particularly with the protagonist's lineage, Chapter 1), and he includes many imaginary titles when he lists the books in the library;
- language.

Speech and language

<u>A constant stream of words</u>

Language is vitally important in Rabelais' writing. His characters have an uncontrollable need to talk, and they do so in a rapid, disordered way: their speech is verbiage, as is the case when Gargantua is mourning his wife (Chapter 3). As a general rule, everything serves as a pretext for an explanation (Pantagruel's birth and name) or a list (the contents of Panurge's bags). Rabelais constantly uses dialogue and quotations, which make the text longer. He also uses coarse, colloquial language, and does not think twice about directly addressing the reader ("Listen now, you ass-pizzles", p. 208). All these techniques breathe life into the text.

<u>Languages</u>

Like many of his fellow humanists, Rabelais believed that language is the foundation of education. Indeed, without language, man has no humanity and is no better than an animal. However, it is not enough to know a single language: besides Latin, basic languages such as Greek and Hebrew are also necessary. Rabelais believes that language should be simple and correct, and he mocks the incomprehensible gibberish of the Limousin student which mixes French and Latin. Panurge, who is a real polyglot, is depicted as a model of linguistic knowledge.

<u>Language as a tool for laughter</u>

For Rabelais, language is also a source of comedy. The author does not hesitate to use crude, coarse language centred on the lower parts of human anatomy to make the reader laugh: he talks about "bollocks" (p. 17), "pricks" (p. 82) and "cocks" (ibid.), for example. Even the use of dialect serves as a pretext to employ vulgar words (the men of Luçon call the first bell of matins "Scratch-your-balls", p. 137). He also uses scatological vocabulary, meaning words that refer to excrement: for example, he frequently employs words like "piss" (ibid.), "fart" (p. 81) and "shit" (p. 33).

Furthermore, Rabelais uses the full range of language to provoke laughter. In this way, he creates far-fetched etymologies: for example, he gives an outlandish explanation of the origin of the names of places where sources of hot water are located. He also likes to have fun with language by parodying jargon (Chapters 12 and 13), using wordplay (Chapter 7) and coining new words.

Religion

Throughout the story, Rabelais denounces the excesses of Christianity (such as the sale of indulgences which reduce or eliminate the punishments Christians face for their sins) or deviations from the true faith (the constant recourse to saints). However, in spite of his many criticisms of religion, Rabelais is not anti-religion: he himself was a member of two religious orders. Furthermore, we must remember that in the 16th century it was impossible to think outside the religious framework.

In the novel, the character of Pantagruel illustrates Rabelais' ideas on this subject, particularly when he prays before his battle with Loup Garou (Chapter 29). In this speech, it appears that:

- man must trust God and act according to His orders;
- God only tolerates war in defence (in this way, Rabelais criticises the wars of conquest waged by France, England and the Holy Roman Empire);
- only a pure Gospel (meaning one without the interpretations of previous commentators or translation errors) should be preached.

Furthermore, Rabelais criticises Medieval glosses (the commentaries of monks in the Middle Ages) and advocates returning to the original languages of the Bible such as Greek and Hebrew in order to understand Christian doctrine and stay closer to its original meaning.

In the 16th century, many scholars adopted the concepts of evangelism. This movement originated in European humanist circles following the rediscovery of texts from Antiquity. As they tried to rigorously edit the texts, they became aware of copying errors in the text of the Bible and of bad translations which had circulated. These authors therefore encouraged returning to the original text and learning ancient languages in order to better understand the biblical stories.

A parody of the chivalric romances

While Rabelais presents his book as a chronicle in the prologue and at the end, we quickly realise that it is in fact a parody of chivalric romances which recounts the "horrifying deeds and exploits of Pantagruel" (p. 13).

The term "chivalric romance" originally referred to prose works in languages such as Old French, Anglo-Norman, Occitan and Provençal (as opposed to Latin) adapted from stories about courtly love and the *chansons de geste* of the 11th and 12th centuries. Because of their origins, chivalric romances resemble the epics of Antiquity depicting the adventures of mythological heroes. Chivalric romances focus on a knight, his adventures and his love affairs, and feature fantastic elements. Other characteristic elements of this genre include the importance attached to genealogy and lineage, the opposition of two communities over a territory, and the opposition between good and evil.

Pantagruel has many similarities with the chivalric romances:

- The intervention of the supernatural: it tells the story of a giant from Utopia (the word literally means "no place").
- The reader follows the exploits of the hero all over France and elsewhere (moving a very heavy bell; fighting Loup Garou, Chapter 29) and his love affairs (Chapter 26).
- Pantagruel's family tree is outlined in the first chapter, and as soon as he gets to Poitiers he visits the grave of a distant ancestor (Chapter 5).
- The battle between Pantagruel and Loup Garou, who invaded Utopia, recalls the Crusades, a recurring theme in the *chansons de geste*. This impression is strengthened by the fact that Pantagruel, symbolising the Christian soldier, appeals to God, while Loup Garou prays to Muhammed.

Rabelais' choice of this genre can be explained by the chivalric romances' resounding success with the public and their large circulation thanks to printing. Furthermore, in Italy (which Rabelais visited on several occasions), epics, particularly those of Ariosto (1474-1533), were very popular. Rabelais was therefore writing for an audience who knew this type of novel well and would undoubtedly compare them with *Pantagruel*.

However, Rabelais did not simply take up the chivalric romance as it was: he parodied it. His aim was not to ridicule Medieval literature, but to reuse the features of chivalric romances in an original way to create a new fictional genre which fused reality and fiction, chronicle and novel.

FURTHER REFLECTION

SOME QUESTIONS TO THINK ABOUT...

- Explain the role of Gargantua's letter in the book. What does it refer to? In light of this chapter and the book as a whole, what does "Science without conscience is but the ruination of the soul" (p. 49) mean? In what way does this summarise Rabelais' ideas?
- What role or roles do languages and words play in *Pantagruel*? Why does Rabelais attach so much importance to them?
- How does Rabelais try to avoid censorship? What advice does he give his reader?
- Why do specialists talk about "popular culture" and "learned culture" in Rabelais' writing? Illustrate your answer using examples.
- How would you describe laughter in Rabelais' writing? What subjects is it used for? What are the author's aims in using this approach?
- In the final chapter, the narrator addresses "Pantagruelists". Who are they? What ideas do they defend? Explain your answer.
- Analyse the pairing of Pantagruel and Panurge. What are the similarities and differences between the two characters? What is their friendship based on?
- Can the novel be described as realistic? Justify your answer.
- In your opinion, why did Rabelais choose to make his hero a giant?

We want to hear from you!
Leave a comment on your online library
and share your favourite books on social media!

FURTHER READING

REFERENCE EDITION

- Rabelais, F. (2006) *Gargantua and Pantagruel*. Trans. Screech, M.A. London: Penguin.

REFERENCE STUDIES

- Bakhtin, M. (2009) *Rabelais and His World*. Bloomington, Indiana: Indiana University Press.
- Merritt, Y. (No date) The Unquenchable Thirst to Understand: Francois Rabelais' Satire of Medieval and Renaissance Learning In 'Gargantua and Pantagruel'. *Ampersand: the science of art; the art of science*. [Online]. [Accessed 3 April 2017]. Available from: <http://itech. fgcu.edu/&/issues/vol2/issue2/rabelais.htm>
- Gioia, T. (No date) 'Gargantua and Pantagruel' by François Rabelais. *Conceptual Fiction*. [Online]. [Accessed 3 April 2017]. Available from: <http://www. conceptualfiction.com/Gargantua_and_Pantagruel. html>
- O'Brien, J. ed. (2010) *The Cambridge Companion to Rabelais*. Cambridge: Cambridge University Press.

MORE FROM BRIGHTSUMMARIES.COM

- Reading guide – *Gargantua* by François Rabelais.

Bright ≡Summaries.com

More guides to rediscover your love of literature

Animal Farm
BY GEORGE ORWELL

The Stranger
BY ALBERT CAMUS

Harry Potter and the Sorcerer's Stone
BY J.K. ROWLING

The Silence of the Sea
BY VERCORS

Antigone
BY JEAN ANOUILH

The Flowers of Evil
BY BAUDELAIRE

www.brightsummaries.com

www.brightsummaries.com

Ebook EAN: 9782806295910

Paperback EAN: 9782806298607

Legal Deposit: D/2017/12603/334

Cover: © Primento

Digital conception by Primento, the digital partner of publishers.

Made in the USA
Las Vegas, NV
05 January 2022

40553884R00015